Original title:
Sting Like a Bee

Editor: Jessica Elisabeth Luik
Author: Kene Elistrand
ISBN HARDBACK: 978-9916-86-379-4
ISBN PAPERBACK: 978-9916-86-380-0

Dancing Among Thorns

In a garden wild, where shadows sleep,
Roses bloom in twilight's deep.
Soft petals drift, as stories bind,
While thorns arise in muted kind.

Steps align in a secret waltz,
Whispers trip, yet none repulse.
Grace and peril merge as one,
Beneath the gaze of the setting sun.

A dance of red in twilight's breath,
Petals fall in a silent death.
Yet in the dusk, new echoes born,
Of souls who danced among the thorn.

Echoes of the Wasp

In the silent hush of the amber dawn,
A single wasp doth break the calm.
Wings of shimmer, sharp and bright,
Carving paths through beams of light.

Amidst the blooms, it darts and dives,
Echoes hum where life survives.
Petals tremble, shadows play,
In the dance of night to day.

A whispered threat within the bloom,
Pierces air, a silent boom.
To those who heed its haunting call,
Beware the wasp, lest you fall.

Petals and Venom

In silent meadows, colors blend,
Petals fall where trees ascend.
Whispers of a love once pure,
Now tainted by a venom's lure.

Each bud a promise, each thorn a lie,
Truths are veiled as shadows fly.
Lovers find their hopes undone,
In the arms of the setting sun.

Poisoned heart, yet beauty's claim,
Petals drop in sorrow’s name.
In the dance of love's cruel whim,
Venom flows from hearts within.

Honeyed Agony

Golden rivers through the hive,
Bees in harmony, alive.
Sweetness flows from toil and pain,
Honeyed agony in every vein.

In the labor, joy and strife,
Echoes of their buzzing life.
Each drop a testament of might,
Beneath the sun's enduring light.

Bittersweet in nature's scheme,
Threads of pain in every dream.
Within the hive, a story spun,
Of honeyed agony 'neath the sun.

Sweet and Sharp

In gardens where the roses grow,
A thorn will guard each velvet cloak.
The gentle breath when breezes blow,
Hides needles keen with nature's stroke.

Such paradox in petals fair,
With fragrance soft and whispers sweet.
Yet underneath such tender care,
Lies steel resolve where soft and fierce meet.

To hold them close is to embrace,
The sharp and sweet, the smile and sting.
A lover's kiss with gentle grace,
A sudden bite that makes hearts sing.

The Ambrosial Duelist

In twilight's hush, the swordsman stands,
With nectar's light in steely hands.
At dusk, his blade a glistening strand,
He carves the stars from whispering sands.

In battles fought with grace and poise,
The duel is savored, sweet with noise.
Each clash a symphony's soft deploys,
Binding night sky with daylight joys.

His skill, a dance of ambrosia,
That merges dusk with blush of dawn.
The sword's embrace a sweet euphoria,
As darkness fades with battles won.

Nature's Sentinel

Beneath the ancient canopy,
A guardian stands with timeless might.
The forest whispers secrets free,
To roots that cradle day and night.

Each leaf a sentinel true and bold,
Watching o'er the earth's grand tale.
With every breeze, the stories told,
Of life and death, of wind and sail.

From dawn till dusk, from birth to end,
Nature's sentinel remains.
Protector, sage, and steadfast friend,
In green attire, through sun and rains.

Petal’s Warrior

In battles fought on meadows green,
A warrior clad in floral sheen.
With petals sharp and leaves unseen,
Defends the light, the forest’s queen.

Each thrust of stem, each bloom’s embrace,
A testament of nature’s might.
In daylight’s glare or moon’s soft face,
The warrior stands with pure delight.

Through seasons' change, through storm and sun,
The petal’s warrior guards the land.
In every fight, the victory won,
By strength of bloom and gentle hand.

Golden Guardians

In fields of sunlit splendor,
Where daisies nod and sway,
Golden guardians flutter,
Marking the end of day.

Their wings a burst of summer,
Glistening in the light,
These gentle souls bring comfort,
In the cool embrace of night.

Through meadows wide and open,
They float on whispers' breeze,
Golden guardians, ever watchful,
Among the flowers and the trees.

Venom of the Skies

Beneath the clouds' vast canopy,
Where shadows stretch and grow,
The venom of the skies descends,
With lethal grace and flow.

Dark wings spread wide and fearsome,
Silent as midnight's breath,
Their presence marks the coming,
Of swift and certain death.

In twilight's dimming echo,
Their silent flight begins,
Venom of the skies prevail,
In nature's ruthless spin.

Enchanted Pincers

Down in the ocean's twilight,
Where waves' soft whispers play,
Enchanted pincers dance and weave,
Neath the froth and spray.

Their armor gleams with mystic light,
In hues of azure glow,
With every click and clatter,
A secret tale they show.

Beneath the moon's soft shimmer,
In waters deep and wide,
Enchanted pincers guard the depths,
Where mariners confide.

Petal Protectors

In gardens lush with morning dew,
Where blooms in splendor wake,
Petal protectors stand their guard,
For nature's beauty's sake.

With petals strong and vibrant,
They shield with tender care,
Fragile buds and blossoms,
From storm and tempest's glare.

In every hue and color,
A silent vow they keep,
Petal protectors hold the line,
While all the garden sleeps.

Dancers of Pain

In shadows cast by moonlight's glare,
They twirl in agony, despair.
A ballet born from silent cries,
In nightly dance, true pain belies.

Their feet leave trails of sorrowed ghost,
On stages dark, where shadows boast.
Each pirouette, a whispered woe,
With tears, the world, their wretched show.

Their sullen eyes, dark pools of night,
Hold secrets veiled in twilight's light.
A choreography of grief,
Their movements, solace, disbelief.

In silence, audience remains,
Mesmerized by their phantom chains.
Dancers of pain, they weave their spell,
In darkened halls where shadows dwell.

Harbingers of Honey

In meadows lush, where wildflowers sing,
The air is sweet, the bees take wing.
They flit on whispers of the breeze,
And brush the petals, nature's keys.

Their golden hosts, in hive they rest,
With work they find their greatest quest.
Harvesting nectar, pure and sweet,
In duty's dance, their hearts compete.

The flowers bloom, each day anew,
In colors bright, their beauty true.
With every sip, and every flight,
They herald dawn's tender light.

The skies they paint with amber hues,
And sunlight warms with honeyed news.
Harbingers of sweet delight,
They bless the world, both day and night.

Wings of Vengeance

With feathers dark as shadow's veil,
In silent flight, they tell their tale.
Upon the wind, their anger rides,
In every gust, their wrath abides.

Their eyes, alight with searing flame,
Seek whispered names, rest assured aim.
Upon their wings, a tale unfolds,
Of vengeance carved in ancient molds.

Through forests dense and mountains high,
Their shadows cross the starry sky.
No mercy found within their gaze,
A judgment cast in fiery blaze.

Their wings beat hard, a righteous sound,
For wrongs they seek to thus confound.
With talons sharp, they strike the chord,
Of justice met in dark accord.

Velvet Armor

Upon the fields of dew and green,
A warrior stands, in armor sheen.
With velvet touch, her battles fought,
In silence shrouded, grace is sought.

Her heart a shield, of tender beat,
No iron forged, yet none defeat.
For every blow, she stands so firm,
In soft resolve, her truths affirm.

The world collides with harsh intent,
Yet velvet yields, and storms relent.
Her paths are marked by gentle sway,
A warrior's peace in night and day.

With whispering breeze, her blade does sing,
A quiet strength, a gentle king.
In battles raged, her love does soar,
In velvet armor, fears implore.

A Dance of Barbs

In shadows deep where thorns do twine,
A dance of barbs, both fierce and fine.
They weave and sway, their movements bold,
A tale of strife and stories told.

Their touch is sharp, yet grace imbues,
A deadly waltz in twilight hues.
Each step a blade, each turn a sting,
As thorns in night commence to sing.

Through darkened glade the figures glide,
With hidden wounds they do not hide.
An eerie beauty fills the air,
A dark ballet of thorny hair.

Melody of Venom

A serpentine chant in moonlit night,
A melody of venom's bite.
It winds through hearts with toxic song,
An echo of what's right and wrong.

Each note a pulse of danger's kiss,
A sinuous dance of serpent's hiss.
Yet beauty lurks in lethal tune,
A deadly charm beneath the moon.

In shadows dark where secrets keep,
The venom's song makes lovers weep.
A symphony of whispers sly,
As poisoned dreams in silence lie.

Swift Silent Strike

In fields of still and quiet ground,
The predator's soft steps unbound.
A swift, silent strike, no warning shown,
In twilight's veil, the seeds are sown.

With eyes like ember, gaze intense,
It measures every move, immense.
The prey unwares of silent death,
Each beat a whisper of last breath.

In nature's dance of life and doom,
The strike comes swift from shadowed gloom.
An ancient rhythm, balance fine,
Of hunter's grace and fate's design.

The Pollen-bearer's Challenge

In fields of gold and petaled hue,
The pollen calls, the sky so blue,
A challenge set by nature's whim,
To labor on, our fate to trim.

Through heavy air and currents bold,
We grasp the grains our wings must hold,
From flower's kiss to hive's embrace,
A journey fraught with dainty grace.

Against the wind we steady glide,
With burdens light, yet far and wide,
In unity, our purpose shared,
In every beat, a life declared.

The morning sun, our guide and friend,
Till daylight fades and shadows bend,
Triumphant hums in twilight's ear,
The challenge met, our duty clear.

Duel in the Garden

Beneath the rose and lilac shade,
A buzzing duel is swiftly made,
Two warriors in their striped array,
Engage in combat's heated fray.

Their wings like whispers in the breeze,
Their stings, a flash that none can seize,
In spirals tight, they twist and turn,
As petals fall, the stakes they burn.

Floral scents their senses fill,
As each defends with iron will,
A garden's peace, the prize at risk,
In nature's play, a deadly brisk.

But as the daylight fades to dusk,
Both warriors tire, their anger husk,
They part, a truce in twilight set,
In gardens calm, their paths reset.

Honeyed Valor

In hives of wax and golden light,
The workers toil from morn to night,
In tight-knit ranks, their valor shows,
In every cell, their courage grows.

With nectar sweet, they fill their homes,
Like liquid sun that brightly roams,
Each tiny drop, a tale of toil,
For future days, they guard the spoil.

The queen they serve, her will their creed,
In honeyed oaths, they find their need,
To brave the storms, the seasons hard,
With steadfast hearts, they watch and guard.

Their tiny lives, a grand ballet,
In valor sworn, they find their way,
With each wingbeat, they pledge their might,
In honeyed valor, day and night.

Buzzed Awakening

In morning light, the garden wakes,
A buzz of life, the dawn it takes,
As nature's chorus fills the air,
A newfound pulse ignites the fair.

From nectar's sip to petal's sheen,
The symphony of wings unseen,
A call to arms for pollen's quest,
In every bloom, new hope is best.

The day unfolds in rhythmic hum,
As flowers sway, their nectar's drum,
Each bee a note in morning's song,
In harmony, all day long.

As evening falls, the music fades,
In twilight's arms, the garden shades,
Yet in their dreams, the buzz will stay,
Till dawn anew, another day.

Buzzing Defenders

In vibrant fields where flowers bloom,
Bees patrol with gentle hum,
Guardians of the sweet perfume,
Their tiny wings a steady drum.

From petal’s edge to leafy crest,
They dance with purpose, no distress,
Each tiny flight, a quest, a test,
In nature's arms, they find their rest.

With sun-kissed wings they weave their fate,
A unity, no room for hate,
Their legacy, a golden freight,
In every hive, we celebrate.

Through morning's light, their path is clear,
Defending blooms year after year,
In every buzz, a story dear,
A symphony for us to hear.

As dusk settles with crimson hue,
Their work persists, both old and new,
Buzzing defenders, tried and true,
In nature's bosom, they renew.

Eclipsed by Wings

In twilight’s glow where shadows play,
A fleeting glimpse of wings on sway,
Like whispers of the dying day,
They weave a dance, then fade away.

Eclipsed by wings both swift and slight,
They vanish into coming night,
Their silhouettes, a fleeting sight,
A ballet bathed in silver light.

Beneath the stars, their secrets hide,
In moonlight's grace, they softly glide,
On twilight's breath, they gently ride,
In silence, mysteries collide.

A transient dream upon the breeze,
A murmur through the swaying trees,
Their grace in flight is sure to tease,
Then leave us yearning, ill at ease.

In night's embrace, their whispers sing,
Of stories carried on thin wing,
Eclipsed by time, an endless ring,
Of endless flight and fleeting spring.

Silent Buzzing Shadows

Silent buzzing shadows roam,
Through fields where wildflowers bloom,
In every dusk, their presence known,
A whisper in the evening's gloom.

Their silent wings bring life anew,
To blossoms kissed by morning dew,
An artistry within their queue,
Invisible, yet bold and true.

With silent hums, they paint the skies,
A symphony where nature lies,
In moonlit eves and soft goodbyes,
Their essence in the twilight cries.

Among the stars, they find their grace,
A shadow's dance, a whispered chase,
In every flight, a quiet trace,
Of life and song in nature's face.

Through silent buzzing shadows weave,
A legacy we can't perceive,
Yet in their hums, we dare believe,
A world they touch, then softly leave.

The Secret Sting

In gardens where the roses cling,
A hidden tale of secret sting,
Where buzzing wings in rhythm swing,
A dance of life that summer brings.

Among the blooms, a silent guard,
With swift intent and body hard,
Invisible yet standing shard,
To trespassers, they're ever marred.

Beneath the sun's warm, golden ring,
They filter through, in whispers sing,
With every bloom, their threads they sling,
A warning in the air they fling.

Yet elegance in flight they boast,
A gentle hum, a quiet host,
Their tiny hearts of courage most,
In every hive, a sacred toast.

Oh, secret sting with purpose wise,
Protect your realm beneath the skies,
In every buzz, the world surprise,
With humming grace and soft disguise.

Belligerent Pollinator

In fields of gold and azure skies,
A tiny warrior darts and flies.
With fervor, fury, zeal and might,
He dances in the morning light.

Through petals soft, he weaves and tilts,
With wings that blur in furious jilt.
His mission clear, he carries on,
Until the break of crimson dawn.

The nectar's lure, a siren's call,
He'll fight and brawl and conquer all.
Yet in his haste, he shows his grace,
Leaving beauty in every place.

Floral Duel

Amidst the garden's hush and calm,
Two rivals face with pulsing psalm.
Their wings a blur, their colors bold,
A story ancient, yet retold.

In dappled light where shadows play,
They circle 'round in fierce melee.
Each bloom a prize, each sip a gain,
In the perennial, wild campaign.

Their skirmish brief, yet full of spark,
A duet in the floral park.
And when the eve comes rolling in,
The duelists rest, their nectar win.

Bane of the Blooms

A whisper in the breeze so soft,
The flowers shiver, petals loft.
For here he comes, the bane, the blight,
A tiny force in morning light.

With proboscis keen, he does ensnare,
The sweetest blooms, their sweet despair.
And though he seems so small and slight,
He steals their essence in the night.

Yet even in his fleeting stay,
The blooms prepare for new display.
For nature's cycle, rough and swift,
Ensures each flower gets its gift.

Soldier of Sweetness

In armor bright of golden hue,
He marches through the morning dew.
A noble knight with duty clear,
To spread the joy from year to year.

His battleground, the meadows wide,
Where fragrant blooms and hopes reside.
With every flight, he claims his prize,
Under the watch of endless skies.

Yet every soldier needs repose,
In twilight's hush, his wings will close.
And as the night covers the land,
His work continues, nature's hand.

Winged Warriors

In fields of gold they bear the sky,
Their wings a blur, they buzz on by.
Heroes of hive, they march in flight,
Defenders of dawn, 'til falls the night.

With courage high, they greet the sun,
Their dance, a tale of battles won.
Through fragrant blooms, they heed the call,
No foe too great, no threat too small.

Guardians brave, in unity,
They weave the air with purity.
Through storms and strife, their path is clear,
For hive and queen, they show no fear.

Through summer's heat, winter's chill,
Their spirits strong, their flight steadfast still.
Bound by the cause, a life in the air,
Together they rise, a bond so rare.

So sing, oh bees, your valiant song,
For in your flight, we all belong.
Winged warriors in light you stand,
The keepers of a fertile land.

The Velvet Sting

Among the petals soft and bright,
A shadow moves in morning light.
Velvet cloak and tiny wings,
Beware, beware the sting it brings.

Its mission swift, precise, and true,
A guardian fierce of skies so blue.
In meadows lush and gardens fair,
It moves unseen, with gentle care.

A velvet hush upon the breeze,
Defender of the blossomed trees.
Its warning clear, its purpose strong,
To shield the blooms where it belongs.

With courage pressed into its core,
It guards the nectar and much more.
A velvet warrior, small yet grand,
Protecting beauty with each stand.

So tread with care among the flowers,
Respect the velvet's guarded powers.
For in its sting, a story told,
Of nature's warriors brave and bold.

Ambush of Nectar

In petals deep, ambrosial trap,
The nectar sweet in golden lap.
A silent ambush lies in wait,
For wings a-beating, tempting fate.

In meadows wide, in gardens close,
Disguised as beauty, nature's dose.
The ambush set in fragrant bloom,
A dance with wings, a fated groom.

Into the heart of blooms they dive,
For nectar sweet, they strive and strive.
Yet in the quest, a risk they face,
An ambush set in nature's grace.

The lure of nectar, pure and bright,
Entices bees in day and night.
But in the bloom, a secret lei,
That ambush waits, a hunter's play.

Oh, bees of gold and velvet hue,
Navigate with wisdom true.
For in the blossom's tender care,
An ambush of nectar waits to snare.

Guardians of the Hive

In shadowed woods, in gardens fair,
A legion moves with tender care.
Guardians of the hive they be,
Protectors strong of queen and bee.

Each dawn they rise with purpose clear,
To shield and serve, with love sincere.
Their wings a shield, their bodies brave,
Each day, each breath, a life they save.

Through golden fields, through silken blooms,
They weave a dance with sweet perfumes.
Their task a bond of loyalty,
Guardians of the hive's decree.

By moon's soft light or sun's bright gleam,
They guard the hive, fulfill the dream.
A world of honey, safe and true,
Built by the many, begun by few.

So honor them, these valiant few,
Their sacrifice for skies so blue.
Guardians of the hive they are,
Our world's protectors, near and far.

Thorn Defender

With shadows cast by ancient thorn,
A valiant heart stands tall and sworn,
To guard the grove with silent pride,
Where whispered secrets softly glide.

An armor forged by night's embrace,
Reflects the moon's enchanting grace,
With every step, a mournful hymn,
Through tangled woods, both dark and dim.

A gaze that pierces through the veil,
With memories that faintly trail,
The past and present intertwine,
In realms where dreams and fears align.

With every thorn, a tale is spun,
Of battles won and shadows run,
A sentinel, forever bound,
To keep the night on hallowed ground.

In twilight's glow, the defender stands,
A guardian carved by nature's hands,
Silent echoes of the night,
In the land where dreams take flight.

Royal Buzz

In gardens rich with summer's bloom,
A monarch dances through the room,
With golden wings that catch the light,
In midday's warmth and eve's delight.

The buzzing whispers through the air,
An orchestra beyond compare,
Each petal bowed in pure respect,
To nature's king, a gem bedecked.

Amidst the flowers, sweet and mild,
The royal scepter, nature's child,
Bestows its favor with a kiss,
On blossoms waiting in sheer bliss.

The hive, it thrives with regal care,
A kingdom vast, beyond compare,
With colonies in perfect tune,
To rhythms of the sun and moon.

In every flutter, grace defined,
A legacy with fate entwined,
The bee, a sovereign of the skies,
In nature's grand, eternal ties.

Tipped with Gold

As dawn unveils the colors bold,
The sky is tipped with hues of gold,
Each ray of light a whispered song,
That brings the earth where dreams belong.

The morning dew on leaves it clings,
Reflects the sun’s expansive wings,
A tapestry in threads of light,
Unfolds the magic of the night.

With every breath, a world anew,
The golden dawn, a sacred view,
Where shadows fade and spirits rise,
Beneath the ever-watching skies.

The meadows bathe in morning's hue,
A palette bright, both old and new,
As nature paints with brushstrokes fine,
The moments where the heavens shine.

In quiet whispers of the morn,
The day is wrapped, in gold adorn,
A promise kept, a story told,
In dawn’s embrace, tipped with gold.

Force of the Hive

In unity, the hive does surge,
A tidal force, a single urge,
With purpose clear, they build and strive,
Together strong, they stay alive.

In bustling dance, they share the tale,
Of blooms and fields, a scented trail,
With every wingbeat, knowledge flows,
In harmony, the wisdom grows.

From dawn till dusk, they toil and buzz,
In nature's grand, resounding hum,
Each role embraced with fervent might,
In golden hues of morning light.

A geometric symphony,
Of hexagons in majesty,
The force of hive, in perfect tune,
Beneath the sun, beneath the moon.

The hive, it breathes, a living being,
In endless cycles, always seeing,
A testament to life's grand scheme,
In every drop of honeyed dream.

Thorned Wings

In twilight's whisper, shadows sing,
Upon the ground, the roses cling.
With thorned wings, they rise and fall,
Through midnight's hush, they heed the call.

Beneath the moon's silver crest,
Where dreams and nightmares find their rest.
A flight of petals, sharp and sewn,
Their beauty hides a cry unknown.

In gardens where the darkness feeds,
The thorned wings dance among the reeds.
A silent wail in flight’s embrace,
A fleeting, painful interlace.

Morning breaks with softened light,
Yet echoes of their night-bound flight.
Their journey, carved in shadows deep,
In hearts of stone, such secrets keep.

Though dawn may come with gentle air,
The thorned wings' tale is never fair.
For beauty sharp, with yearning sings,
A haunting dance on thorned wings.

Silent Swarm

Beneath a sky both dark and deep,
A silent swarm begins to creep.
With whispered winds, they glide and sway,
Through shadows soft, they find their way.

No buzz or hum to mark their flight,
Just ghostly wings in endless night.
An unseen force, a clouded form,
They drift, they whirl—this silent swarm.

In quietude, their presence weaves,
Through twilight's hush, beneath the leaves.
An ode to stillness, they perform,
A dance unknown—this silent swarm.

Whispered secrets, cold and gray,
In silence, they will find their sway.
An empty whisper in the storm,
Unheard, unseen—this silent swarm.

And as the day succumbs to dusk,
Their presence slips into the musk.
A fleeting murmur, unadorned,
A phantom's dream—this silent swarm.

Golden Echoes

In the dawn's first tender light,
Golden echoes take to flight.
With whispers soft, they paint the morn,
In hues of day's most silent adorn.

From fields of gold, their voices rise,
A chorus grand beneath the skies.
Each glint and gleam, a tale retold,
In echoes bright, both young and old.

Through valleys deep and mountains high,
Their shining words continue to fly.
To hearts they send their warming glow,
In softest tones, their secrets flow.

Though fleeting as the morning's breath,
These echoes banish night's cold death.
With every beam, a promise made,
In golden trust, their flight displayed.

So as the day begins anew,
The golden echoes whisper through.
To every soul, they gently sing,
A timeless warmth each dawn to bring.

Secrets of the Hive

In a world of sweetest scent,
Secrets of the hive are spent.
With every buzz and busy hum,
Their whispered tales so softly come.

Among the nectar's rich delight,
They gather stories day and night.
With honeyed words and dances clear,
They share their secrets far and near.

In cells of wax, their lore is kept,
Guarded close where dreams have slept.
Each drop of gold from flower to comb,
A legacy within their home.

Through meadows wide and forests dense,
Their wisdom flows without pretense.
To every bloom, they lend their grace,
In nature's heart, they find their place.

So listen close, and you may find,
The hive’s sweet truths within your mind.
A hidden world both vast and live,
Unveils itself, the secrets of the hive.

Avenger in Black and Gold

In realms where shadows lay so cold,
A hero rises, fierce and bold.
With wings alight, and vengeance near,
The avenger stirs, dispelling fear.

Cloaked in black with bands of gold,
Stories of might and valor unfold.
Across the fields, in meadows vast,
Echoes of legends from the past.

Guardians watch as wings take flight,
Against the dark, a beacon of light.
The avenger soars, through wind and time,
In songs and whispers, the bees' own rhyme.

With pollen dust upon his quest,
He guards the weak, defends the nest.
An emblem strong, through day and night,
The avenger shows his radiant might.

In every bloom, in morning's breath,
He dances on the edge of death.
For life anew, in gold and black,
The avenger leads; there's no turning back.

Hymns of the Pollen Guard

On breeze and bloom, the guardians sing,
Vibrations felt on every wing.
Their chorus hums through fields of green,
A symphony forever keen.

In golden light and petals bright,
Protecting life with all their might.
They weave their songs, both old and new,
Bind the day with morning dew.

Buzzing tales through fragrant air,
Stories of their valiant care.
In harmony with blossoms' grace,
Guardians hold this sacred space.

Pollen guards with fervent pride,
In each safeguard, faith's their guide.
Every hymn, a promise made,
To shelter all, unscathed, unswayed.

From dawn till dusk, their vigil kept,
In silent nights when all have slept.
The hymns they sing, both bold and kind,
A testament to strength combined.

Celestial Pollinator

In cosmic realms, where stardust glows,
A figure dances, ebb and flow.
Celestial wings in twilight's gleam,
A pollinator's timeless dream.

Across the void, in silent flight,
Guided by the astral light.
Through galaxies, through endless night,
Spreads life and wonder, pure delight.

In flowered orbs, on distant plains,
The celestial beauty reigns.
Pollen trails through space engraved,
In this vast universe, life is saved.

Every bloom, a star's rebirth,
A symbol of the endless worth.
Of the celestial being's lore,
Creating life forevermore.

In cosmic silence, whispers sweet,
The pollinator's secret beat.
A rhythm pulsing, pure and grand,
Embracing all in star-clad hand.

Whispers of the Hive

Within the hive, a secret told,
Whispers weave a story bold.
In honeyed halls where shadows hide,
A vibrant, thriving world resides.

Buzzing voices, soft and clear,
Convey tales we seldom hear.
Of unity and trust so fine,
Bound by ties of ancient line.

From queen to worker, drone to king,
They share the weight of everything.
A dance of life, of purpose sure,
Each role revered, each duty pure.

In every cell, a memory holds,
Whispers of the young and old.
Of seasons past and blossoms bright,
Of nights endured and days of light.

With every hum, the secrets blend,
A promise made to keep, defend.
For within the hive, the whispers stay,
A song of life in sweet array.

Honey and Hurt

Golden rivers, sweet delight,
Morning sun through trees alight,
Nature's gentle, calm embrace,
Hidden dangers in each place.

Bees will dance in sunlight's glow,
Secrets in their flight they show,
Beneath the flowers, shadows play,
Sweetness guards the thorny way.

In honey's taste, a comfort found,
Yet hidden costs can oft astound,
For in the sweetness lies a sting,
Duality in everything.

Hurt will linger, whisper close,
Balance tips, as knowledge grows,
Life's ambrosia, bittersweet,
Every triumph, fears repeat.

Embrace the nectar, taste its song,
Understand where you belong,
Among the flowers, joys you'll learn,
Honey and hurt, forever burn.

Whispers of the Swarm

In the field, the buzz begins,
Silent calls above the din,
Whispers float on summer's air,
Secrets that the swarms do share.

Tiny wings in unison fly,
Patterns etched against the sky,
Mysteries in their paths concealed,
Language that will not be revealed.

Shadows cast by countless drones,
Voices deep in buzzing tones,
Nature’s code, encrypted tight,
Spoken through the day and night.

Listen close, they tell a tale,
Of resilience, life’s travail,
Echoes of a world unseen,
In the space where bees convene.

Their whispers hold the fragile world,
In their wings, a future’s swirled,
Swarm's soft song, a hopeful sign,
Intertwined with yours and mine.

Razor in the Garden

Blossoms blush in morning light,
Petals soft and dewdrops bright,
But hidden there in colors warm,
Lies the shape of nature’s harm.

Amidst the greens, a glint revealed,
Danger harnessed, secrets sealed,
Razor sharp and silent death,
Lurking close with bated breath.

Beauty dressed in gentle guise,
Threads of peril, sleek disguise,
In the garden’s tranquil bloom,
Lie the seeds of subtle doom.

Caution walks with tender grace,
Through the verdant, hidden space,
Eyes alert to every snare,
Seeking safety, finding where.

Even in this Eden vast,
Tempests rage and shadows cast,
Razor edges cut the trust,
Garden's peace turns into dust.

Songs of the Sting

In the meadows, whispers bring,
Songs of creatures with a sting,
Melodies that weave through air,
Warning all who venture there.

Bees compose the symphony,
With their hum, a warning plea,
Guardians of their golden troves,
Hidden in the hallowed groves.

Every note, a lesson taught,
In their dance, a wisdom sought,
Danger in the sweetest bloom,
Life and death in subtle loom.

Singers small with mighty might,
Crafting songs both day and night,
Offering their precious gift,
Till the shadows start to lift.

Listen close, the song’s begun,
Old as time and twice as spun,
In the sting, the truth you'll find,
In the song, the threads unwind.

The Apiarist's Ace

In fields where golden blooms abound,
An apiarist's touch is found.
With careful hands, he courts the grace,
Of bees that roam a fragrant place.

His gentle hums and quiet calls,
Guide winged dancers through the halls.
Sweet nectar found in nature's lace,
All hail the apiarist's ace.

In evening's glow, they flutter home,
A world within the wicker dome.
He tends the hive with calm embrace,
In honeyed peace, no sign of haste.

Each drop of gold a labor's prize,
Reflects the light of azure skies.
Through seasons' turn, his heart remains,
Forever bound to bees' refrains.

With wisdom old, yet spirits young,
He weaves a song the bees have sung.
In harmony, they interlace,
The magic of the apiarist's ace.

Defender of the Blossom

In gardens rich with petals bright,
A guardian roams both day and night.
His armor, threads of morning dew,
He champions blooms with heart so true.

Among the fragrant, colorful maze,
He stands to ward the withering haze.
With every step, a silent vow,
To shield the blossoms, here and now.

Each flower kissed by golden rays,
Finds strength beneath his watchful gaze.
The winds may rage, the storms may come,
Yet he remains, a steady drum.

No foe too bold, no drought too fierce,
To pierce his heart or break his pierce.
For he, the bloom’s most trusted knight,
Defends its beauty through the night.

So bloom and blossom, bright and fast,
For he shall guard till breath's last.
A silent hero, in shadow's glen,
Defender of the blossom then.

Hive's Precision

In symphonies of amber hues,
The hive is where precision brews.
Each worker bee, on sacred mission,
Attests to nature's fine precision.

From dawn until the twilight's fall,
They dance within the hexagon’s hall.
With perfect care and true division,
They build the hive with keen precision.

No effort wasted, nor misplaced,
In this, a kingdom interlaced.
Every buzz, a calculation,
In service of their sweet creation.

Pollen gathered, nectar stored,
All duties met, none ignored.
Through unity and shared vision,
They celebrate the hive's precision.

In waxy halls and honeyed gleams,
The hive is more than what it seems.
A testament through each incision,
To nature's art and grand precision.

Sweetness with a Punch

In blossoms where the nectar hides,
A tale of sweetness long abides.
The honeyed art with subtle crunch,
A story of sweet punch.

The bees collect, with rhythmic flair,
Their bounty from the fragrant air.
Elixirs born with springtime's bunch,
Their labor yields a sweetened punch.

In golden jars, the treasure lies,
A syrup of the sunlit skies.
Yet deeper lies, beneath the hunch,
A depth of flavor’s gentle punch.

From comb to jar, the journey winds,
In twists of nature's grand designs.
Every drop, a world to launch,
On tongues, a burst of sweetened punch.

So savor slow, and taste the bloom,
In winter’s chill or summer's plume.
With each delight, a joyful crunch,
The gift of nature's sweetened punch.

Guardians in Flight

Beneath the twilight's gentle shade,
Guardians in flight, silently parade.
Wings of dusk, a feathery guise,
Gliding through the moonlit skies.

Silent whispers in the air so cold,
Stories of bravery, ancient and bold.
Their eyes gleam bright, a guiding light,
In the stillness of the endless night.

They vow to shield the dreams we keep,
A promise carved in sleep so deep.
With every beat and every sigh,
They bind the stars in night's dark sky.

Through storms and mist, their path they trace,
Guardians of an untamed space.
Above the world where shadows blend,
Their flight, a timeless message to send.

In realms unseen, they find their way,
A dance of hope till break of day.
With every dawn, the dreams alight,
Guardians in flight, from night to light.

Thorned Guardians

Thorned guardians watch and wait,
At twilight's door, they seal the gate.
In gardens wild, their echoes lie,
Protectors of where secrets hide.

Their presence felt in moonlit gloom,
Defiant thorns in silent bloom.
A promise made in petals fair,
Guardians with a tender care.

Amid their touch, a gentle sting,
To lullaby the lonely spring.
Each thorn and petal, night and day,
In vigil ever strong, they stay.

Their purpose clear, their gaze intense,
To shield the heart from each offense.
With every thorn, a fortress stands,
Guardians crafted by nature's hands.

In every rose, a tale unfolds,
Of love and fear in whispers told.
Thorned guardians, the shadows play,
In gardens where the heart may stray.

Sweeter Than Pain

In twilight's hush, a secret lies,
A bitter truth beneath the skies.
Yet in the heart where sorrow stains,
There blooms a love, sweeter than pain.

From every tear that softly falls,
A melody within us calls.
With aching steps, a dance we trace,
Through shadowed alleys, time's embrace.

In every bruise, a tenderness,
An echo of a lost caress.
Yet in the depths where sorrows reign,
Love lingers long, sweeter than pain.

With every wound, a chance to mend,
A tale of hope that doesn't end.
For in the dark, a light remains,
A beacon bright, sweeter than pain.

In life's embrace, where grief may tread,
Where whispering ghosts of past are fed.
We find a strength, a sweet refrain,
A love that's bound, sweeter than pain.

Humming with Fury

In stormy skies where dark clouds form,
The air ignites with nature’s storm.
A whisper born in tempest’s rise,
A humming fury, fire in disguise.

Amid the gale, a power coils,
Unseen forces, the world embroils.
With thunder's roar and lightning’s gaze,
A symphony of nature's blaze.

In every crash and every boom,
A tale of wrath begins to bloom.
Yet in the eyes of stormy night,
Lie secrets in the thunder’s might.

The ground does tremble at its call,
An echo’s dance through nature’s hall.
With every pulse and every flare,
Feel the fury humming in the air.

A force unbridled, wild and free,
It speaks of power we cannot see.
Humming with fury, fierce, untamed,
Its song, a force we cannot name.

Sweet Shieldbearer

Upon the battlefield, hearts intertwine,
A guardian's love, pure and divine,
With armor gleaming, forever to defend,
The tender touch that fears can mend.

A sentinel, whose strength endures,
Compassion's blade pierces and cures,
In shadows deep, the light they'd bring,
Their soul, a fortress, unwavering spring.

Through blood and tear, their vow remains,
A promise etched in love's sweet chains,
For in each clash, a kiss of grace,
A shieldbearer's serene, tender embrace.

War's cacophony, yet they stand tall,
Against each rage, each fateful call,
Gentle hearts in armored guise,
A moonlit glow to battle's skies.

With every clash, their song resounds,
In silence speaks, where love abounds,
A beacon, 'midst the cold and strife,
Sweet shieldbearer guards with life.

Zephyr of the Garden

In the garden, breezes play,
Whispering secrets of the day,
Softly swaying, leaves do dance,
In the zephyr's tender trance.

Petals flutter, colors bright,
As the wind bestows its light,
A gentle touch, a lover’s hand,
Caressing blooms across the land.

Each blossom nods, a silent call,
Responding to the zephyr’s thrall,
In this sweet, eternal waltz,
Nature writes in whispers' vaults.

Through branches weave, with grace and cheer,
A song of love for all to hear,
Zephyr kisses, softly sewn,
Bind the heart to Nature’s tone.

In the stillness, midst the green,
Lies the magic, softly seen,
For where the zephyr breathes anew,
Dreams are born in morning dew.

Petal's Protector

Amidst the garden, stern and grand,
A guardian takes its solemn stand,
To shield each petal from the storm,
And keep its colors pure and warm.

Through rain and wind, it does not yield,
A steadfast heart, a nature's shield,
With roots deep in the fertile ground,
It fights for blooms all year ‘round.

In sunlit days, it casts its grace,
A shadowed haven, a tranquil place,
For petals delicate and dear,
It guards the beauty, fierce yet near.

No storm too wild, no sun too bright,
To challenge this protector's might,
For in its heart, a vow holds true:
To nurture life in every hue.

Though seasons change and time may drift,
Its love and care forever lift,
Petal's protector, strong you stand,
A sentinel of Nature's hand.

Resonance of War Wings

With wings of steel and hearts of flame,
They soar through skies that know no name,
In echoes loud, their presence felt,
As heralds of the fates long dealt.

Above the fray, in endless flight,
They dance with honor, day and night,
A spectral force, a timeless choir,
Their voice a roar, a song of fire.

Through clouds they pierce, with thunder keen,
Upon the battlefield, they gleam,
Each beat a rhythm, fierce and wild,
The war wings echo, tempest styled.

In silent dawn or dusk's embrace,
Their shadows cast a haunting grace,
For every clash and every cry,
Resonates through the open sky.

Their legacy, a tale of might,
Written in the endless flight,
War wings carry through the storm,
A fierce resolve, in battle's form.

Honeycomb Vigilante

In the quiet of the midnight hush,
A vigilante in golden armor's gleam,
Guards the treasure, sweet and lush,
Awake in an eternal dream.

With wings that hum an urgent tale,
Through moonlit fields they glide,
Their resolve never to pale,
In shadows where dangers hide.

Nature's keeper, fierce and mild,
Defender of the waxen wall,
Protector of the nectar wild,
They heed the hive's call.

Each cell a fortress, strong and bold,
Crafted with precision and grace,
In their bounty, tales unfold,
A sanctuary, a sacred place.

Oh, Honeycomb Vigilante brave,
In your watch, the world does thrive,
For in the treasures that you save,
Our sweetest dreams come alive.

Hive's Knight

In the perennial quest for bloom,
To golden realms unseen they flee,
A knight in the hive's perfumed room,
Sworn to loyalty's decree.

Armored in a sunlit hue,
They traverse the fragrant breeze,
Through skies crystal and blue,
A journey without cease.

Duty echoes in each beat,
Guardians of a secret lore,
Where honey and heart do meet,
At nature's core.

Warrior in the pollen war,
Shield of the fragile flower,
Defending peace along the spoor,
With relentless, tireless power.

Ours is a world they daily save,
In their ceaseless, gentle flight,
We owe our blooms, our sweet enclave,
To the hive's eternal knight.

Guardian of the Honeyed Ream

A realm resplendent, swathed in gold,
Deep within the hive's embrace,
Where stories of the nectar told,
Sing of guardians' grace.

Through verdant fields they roam and dive,
Each petal's secret sought,
Guardian of the hive's sweet thrive,
In every bloom they've wrought.

Rippled sunlight tracks their flight,
Mapping out the day's long quest,
In softest dawn or dusky twilight,
They guard their home, their rest.

Every drop of honey found
Is their siege weapon, their praise,
As they flit from ground to ground,
In their golden maze.

Oh, noble sentinels, kind and brave,
May your journey never cease,
For in your fevered, tireless save,
We find beauty, we find peace.

Golden Arbiter

In a realm where sunlight spills,
Upon blooms in dawn's first light,
Arbiter of the golden frills,
Rules in silent, steady might.

With wings that shimmer, whisper pale,
They weigh the scales of pollen fate,
Their judgments never fail,
Balancing nature's plate.

From flower unto flower they glide,
In their quest for fragrant truth,
With justice as their guide,
In the sweetness of their youth.

Each judgment shaped in amber clear,
Every decree in nectar's name,
Their path is one we hold dear,
In their golden fame.

O Golden Arbiter, fair and true,
In your care, the garden thrives,
Nature's harmony built anew,
Within your vigilant hives.

Kissed by Venom

A whisper spreads from lips of dread,
In twilight's grasp, so near the end,
A toxin sweet as lovers' thread,
Where shadows drink and sorrows blend.

Enchanted sin in moonlight's shade,
A stolen breath, a wish unmade,
Her eyes confess the secrets laid,
By serpents dark in night’s parade.

No cure exists for poison bared,
The venom kissed, and hearts ensnared,
A dance of pain, a spell declared,
Where dreams dissolve and fate is dared.

She spoke of love in tongues of stone,
A curse entwined, forever known,
Now lost within her chilling groan,
Two souls adrift, a darkness grown.

Flowery Fortress

Within the garden's quiet clasp,
Where petals guard the silent pass,
A fortress blooms in colors vast,
To hold the heart in fragrant mass.

Each blossom whispers tales of old,
In hues of pink, in reds so bold,
Their secrets told in bouquets sold,
And stories sung in shades of gold.

Through thorns, the guarded soul may tread,
To find a solace where it's led,
Within this worlds, where fears are shed,
And tranquil dreams can sweetly spread.

A citadel in nature's keep,
Protected by the vows we keep,
To bloom in beauty, quiet and deep,
In floral strength and whispered sleep.

Beneath the Buzz

The meadow hums with life and grace,
Where bees in golden search embrace,
A dance of nectar's sweetened chase,
Beneath the buzz, a hidden place.

In gentle murmurs, whispers grow,
Amongst the blooms by rivers flow,
The sunlight pours a tender glow,
And nature paints its vibrant show.

With wings so swift, they weave the air,
A melody beyond compare,
Their journey's song, a silent prayer,
In harmony, without despair.

Beneath the buzz, the world seems still,
A tranquil wash o'er vale and hill,
In every beat, a quiet thrill,
Of life's relentless, tender will.

Cloaked in Honey

Enrobed in gold, the sweetness found,
In amber pools where dreams abound,
A silken cloak with which hearts are crowned,
From nature's lap, such gifts unbound.

Beneath the sun's caress so fair,
The bees craft art with loving care,
In every drop, their soul's declare,
A treasure rich beyond compare.

To taste the warmth of flower's kiss,
In honeyed streams of liquid bliss,
A memory of nature's tryst,
Held in each golden, soothing miss.

Cloaked in honey, time stands still,
A nectar's balm for life's own chill,
In every sweet, a gentle thrill,
A promise kept in nature's will.

Insects of Iron

Insects of iron with gleaming shell,
Underneath the moon's faint spell,
Whispers of gears in twilight's blend,
Unveiling secrets they defend.

Clockwork hearts in rhythmic song,
To nature's symphony they belong,
Metallic wings in silent flight,
Gliding through the endless night.

Machinery with a lifelike grace,
Navigating space with little trace,
Their tales in rust and oil are spun,
Untold stories one by one.

Glistening under starlit beams,
Fitting pieces from ancient dreams,
Insects of iron roam the air,
Mechanical life beyond compare.

Wind and wire, fuse and frame,
In the shadows, they remain,
Creators of the quiet rune,
Dancing in the pale-lit moon.

Golden Torment

Upon the field where shadows cry,
A glint of gold ignites the sky,
The heart feels joy, then swift restrain,
In golden torment, love and pain.

Through the silent winds they call,
Memories built to rise and fall,
Chains of amber, holding tight,
An endless cycle of delight.

In shimmering hues that light the way,
Dreams in torment often sway,
Flames that both burn bright and cold,
Secrets in their depths unfold.

Hearts entwined in golden strife,
Moments dancing, pulse and knife,
Each breath a blend of sweet despair,
Heading towards a destined snare.

Still, we chase the gilded light,
Through tunnels of both wrong and right,
For in the torment, truths reside,
And lovers find the strength to bide.

Beneath the Honeycomb

Beneath the honeycomb's sweet veil,
Lies a secret, gentle tale,
Of whispers in the amber flow,
Where golden dreams in twilight glow.

Soft murmurs echo through the hive,
Keeping ancient lore alive,
Nature's poetry on wings,
In every cell, a story sings.

The labyrinth of love and light,
Crafted in the soft night's bite,
Drizzles down in nectar's gold,
Treasures that the shadows hold.

Silent workers in the dark,
Creating symphonies so stark,
Their artistry both fierce and mild,
Sophistication, nature's child.

In those depths where sweetness churns,
A world of wonders twists and turns,
Beneath the honeycomb, they weave,
Life's tender touch we cannot leave.

Serrated Wings

With serrated wings in darkened flight,
Across the sky, they pierce the night,
In sharp patterns, shadows play,
A dance of whispers, swift and gray.

Feathers edged like blades so fine,
Cut through silence, intertwine,
Each motion holds a secrets' key,
A call to souls who dare to see.

Specters of the twilight gleam,
In serrated wings, they dream,
Tales of sorrow, love, and woe,
Captives of the night’s soft glow.

Through the mist, they navigate,
Bound by fate's intricate gate,
Wings of silver, dark as coal,
Carving stories from the soul.

In their flight, both fierce and pure,
Echoes promise, soft, unsure,
Serrated wings in moonlit skies,
Guardians of secrets in disguise.

Nectar Nightmares

Beneath the moon's silvery gaze,
In garden's shadowed, darkened phase,
Flowers bloom in spectral light,
Whispering secrets of the night.

Honeyed dreams in petals twined,
Luring both the heart and mind,
But where sweetness lies ahead,
Danger's whispers fill with dread.

Bees that sip the nectar sweet,
Dare to taste the twilight treat,
For every drop that’s softly sipped,
A shadowed tale with darkness dripped.

Dreams of honey turn to fear,
When nightmares in the night appear,
In the heart of blossom's night,
Creeps the shadow’s creeping blight.

Beware the bloom under the moon,
Songs of night in silent croon,
For there lie within the night,
Nectar's nightmares out of sight.

Silent Soldiers

Silent soldiers guard the dawn,
Marching forth as night is gone,
In the woodland, rows they form,
Standing tall in any storm.

Leaves that whisper in a breeze,
Armors clad in hues of green,
Unseen battles these trees wage,
Time and tempest grow their age.

Rooted deep in earth's embrace,
Steadfast in their given place,
Silent soldiers of the land,
Hold the ground on which they stand.

Sunlight crowns their ancient heads,
Morning dew on branches spreads,
Voiceless warriors never tire,
Braving frost and summer's fire.

Guarding secrets of the past,
Through each storm they hold steadfast,
Silent soldiers, brave and bold,
Keep the earth, their duty told.

Poised to Pierce

Poised to pierce the veil of night,
Stars align in silent fight,
Celestial blades in heavens high,
Cut through fabric of the sky.

In the stillness comes their glow,
Silent swords that thousands know,
Guiding mariners in plight,
Through the vast seas' endless night.

Each ray sharp with cosmic sheen,
Sculpting paths where dreams have been,
Charting courses, ancient, new,
In the skies of midnight's blue.

Constellations drawn in gold,
Whisper tales of warriors bold,
Poised to pierce the darkened veil,
Telling fates in starlit trail.

Through the night they illuminate,
Visions passed through heaven’s gate,
Stars untiring watch and dance,
Poised to pierce, to take a chance.

Guardians of Gold

Golden fields beneath the sun,
Harvest time for everyone,
Shadows long in amber grain,
Guardians watching much the same.

Scarecrow stands with empty gaze,
Watching over golden maize,
Sentinel through dusk till dawn,
Silhouette on verdant lawn.

Gold that glimmers in the light,
Guardians through day and night,
Rustling whispers through the breeze,
Pass through rows of standing trees.

In the bounty of the field,
Treasures of the earth revealed,
Guardians of gold stand tall,
Witness to the seasons' call.

Come the harvest rich and pure,
Nature's gifts they do ensure,
Guardians of gold remain,
Watching over endless grain.

Nature's Dagger

Among the leaves so green, it strikes,
A flash of wing, a blur in flight,
With aim precise it takes its prize,
Nature’s dagger, swift and bright.

Silent hunter in the day,
Speckled wing and sharp of beak,
Amidst the foliage it does play,
A rhythm wild, beauty unique.

Through shadowed woods it weaves paths,
Invisible but for keen eyes,
A testament to nature's craft,
A wonder beneath open skies.

No tree too tall, no sky too high,
This perfect hunter reigns on strong,
With talons gripping, wings held wide,
Nature’s balance, a silent song.

A fleeting glimpse, then it is gone,
But memory lingers where it tread,
Nature's dagger, dusk till dawn,
Alive in minds where dreams are fed.

The Buzzing Ballet

In gardens where the flowers bloom,
A tiny dancer starts its play,
With brilliant stripes of black and gold,
The buzzing ballet greets the day.

It flits from petal, sipping sweet,
A zephyr in the warming sun,
Its wings a blur, its mission fleet,
From early morn till day is done.

Each blossom is a partner true,
In this grand dance of life and light,
Pollination's work to do,
From dawn's first glow to soft twilight.

Through air it weaves a magic thread,
Connecting blooms in spring’s embrace,
Ensuring future blossoms spread,
Upon the earth, a painted grace.

With tireless flurry, there it goes,
A symphony so wild and free,
The garden thrives, the cycle flows,
Thanks to the buzzing ballet's glee.

Piercing Through Silence

In the stillness of twilight's fold,
A sound unfurls, both sharp and cold,
An arrow loosed from nature’s bow,
Piercing through silence, soft and bold.

Echoes travel through the night,
Of creatures hidden, out of sight,
Each call and cry a mystery,
A symphony of dark and light.

Amidst shadows, stars take hold,
Silent whispers, truths untold,
But cutting through this veiled repose,
A solitary voice, so bold.

From distant hills or nearby stream,
It wakes the night from tranquil dream,
A poignant note, so pure, pristine,
Piercing through silence like moonbeam.

And when it fades, the quiet falls,
A deeper hush, as night enthralls,
Yet in the heart, a memory gleams,
Of nature's voice and midnight calls.

Buzz in the Breeze

Beneath the summer’s golden rays,
Where meadows sprawl in verdant seas,
A gentle hum begins to play,
The soothing buzz within the breeze.

Among the flowers, colors bright,
This melody takes wing and flight,
From bloom to bloom, it weaves its song,
A choir of bees, where they belong.

With each soft beat of tiny wings,
The harmony of nature rings,
As pollen dances through the air,
Spreading life with tender care.

No grander stage than fields so wide,
Where earth and sky in peace abide,
And in between, this humble tune,
A buzz that carries joy past noon.

So let us sit and softly breathe,
This symphony no hand can weave,
A gentle buzz within the breeze,
A sweet reminder, hearts at ease.

Songs of the Swarm

In twilight’s thrumming glow,
Bees hum their secret psalms.
Winds whisper whispers low,
As dusk enfolds in calms.

Golden hives sing tales,
Of nectar, bloom, and flight.
In the chorus of gales,
They dance from dawn to night.

Pollen tunes they play,
With wings in perfect rhyme.
In fields' vast bouquet,
They craft the floral chime.

The hive's symphonic hum,
Is nature's sweet refrain.
Where bees and blossoms come,
To serenade the plain.

In every petal's fold,
A melody is born.
Through garden tapestries of gold,
Resound the songs of the swarm.

Guardian of the Petals

Amidst the blooming swell,
A sentinel soars high.
Each blossom's tale to tell,
Beneath the watchful sky.

A vigilant embrace,
Protects the garden's grace.
With every bee's soft trace,
In perfumed air and space.

Wings that softly whirr,
Amidst the blooming hue.
Guarding every stir,
Of petals kissed with dew.

Nectar kept in trust,
By a guardian's gentle care.
A promise in twilight's dust,
That every bloom shall fare.

Floral whispers speak,
Of the protector's flight.
In every petal's streak,
Glow the guardians of the night.

The Blossom Guardian

A solstice sentinel,
With wings of amber glow.
Keeps every petal well,
Through summer's ebb and flow.

In gardens lush and wide,
The guardian takes its stand.
Where blossoms open wide,
And thrive by gentle hand.

Each petal is a dream,
A guardian weaves with care.
In sunlight's golden gleam,
Its love is always there.

Through midnight's velvet sheen,
And morning's gentle light.
The guardian is seen,
In shadows soft and bright.

A blossom's silent friend,
In every season's span.
Their bond shall never end,
In nature's tender plan.

Pure Nectar

In flowers' hidden heart,
A treasure lies concealed.
Where blossoms gently part,
Their secrets are revealed.

Drops of sunlight pure,
In petals' tender grasp.
The nectar sweet and sure,
In nature's gentle clasp.

With each gentle kiss,
The bees draw liquid gold.
In soft, harmonious bliss,
This story is retold.

In fields of fragrant bloom,
Where buzzing chorals play.
The nectar finds its room,
Beneath the bright array.

In every flower's core,
A nectar tale does lie.
A sip, a taste, and more,
Beneath the open sky.

Sharp Grief

In shadows deep and cold,
Pain’s whisper is a knife.
A story yet untold,
In the quietude of life.

Tears trace the sharp relief,
Of love that once did bloom.
In the hollow halls of grief,
Echoes a silent gloom.

Memories in shards,
Of moments lost in time.
Wounds like bitter guards,
Sing a mournful rhyme.

In the depth of night,
When stars seem far away.
The ache clings tight,
In sorrow’s endless gray.

Yet through the piercing pain,
A dawn may one day break.
In every lost refrain,
Hope softly stirs awake.

Buzzing in the Battle

Amidst the fields where flowers bloom,
The buzzing warriors take their flight.
With wings that hum a tune of doom,
They charge into the fray so bright.

Their armor glistens in the sun,
A dance of gold upon the breeze.
United, they are all but one,
Against the world, their foes appease.

With every thrust, a life be spared,
Yet battles rage without remorse.
Their stingers sharp, their courage bared,
Through sky and nectar, set their course.

For queen and hive, they will protect,
Each mission bold, where'er they roam.
In nature's balance, they connect,
Forever buzzing, finding home.

The Honeyed Warrior

In golden fields, the sun’s caress,
A warrior with honeyed might.
From dawn to dusk, their fight profess,
To safeguard nectar and the light.

With gentle wings, their power hums,
A melody of life's embrace.
They guard the land where sweet entwines,
With courage written on their face.

Their battles fought with loving grace,
Defending every precious bloom.
A hero in that sacred space,
Against the shadows, casting gloom.

For every drop of golden hue,
They weave a tale of sacrifice.
A testament to all that’s true,
The honeyed warrior, pure and nice.

Dance of the Hive

In synchronized, ethereal flow,
The hive performs its sacred dance.
A ballet where the blossoms grow,
In rhythmic trance, they sure advance.

Each step a story, told in flight,
Communion in the air above.
They craft their world from morning light,
In patterns of collective love.

Their dance defends, their dance sustains,
A symphony of purpose pure.
In togetherness, dissolve the pains,
Ensuring futures will endure.

Through fields of gold, they swirl and glide,
In unity, the hive survives.
A tapestry where dreams abide,
The dancers' truth forever thrives.

Amber-Armored Gladiator

With armor cast in amber's glow,
The gladiator braves the fray.
In battles fought through ebb and flow,
Defending life by night and day.

Vociferous wings that never tire,
A sentinel of floral plains.
Their courage burns with fierce aspire,
In golden hues that break the chains.

They march in ranks, no fear to show,
Against the odds, they hold their might.
In every flight, their spirits grow,
Through trials vast, they claim their right.

With each return, the hive they praise,
Their sacrifice not given light.
In amber's hues and morning rays,
These gladiators anchor the night.

Whispers in the Air

Soft breezes carry tales of yore,
Across the fields, beyond the shore.
In secret tongues, they gently share,
The mysteries of earth and air.

Leaves rustle with a knowing grace,
Conspiring whispers, face to face.
They tell of love and silent care,
In whispered tones, for all to hear.

The night holds secrets in its fold,
Stories of stardust, bright and bold.
In every gust, in every sway,
The whispers in the air convey.

From dawn till dusk, they gently sing,
Of seasons' turn and bird on wing.
In harmony, they weave their fare,
A tapestry of whispers in the air.

Each whisper holds a world unseen,
A fleeting dream, a glistening sheen.
In quiet moments, if you dare,
You'll hear the whispers in the air.

Nectar's Nemesis

In gardens lush, where blooms abound,
A quiet battle, without sound.
The bloomless bee, in desperate plight,
Seeks nectar's sweet, elusive light.

Amidst the petals, bright and fair,
The sprays of color, unaware.
The bee's lament, a silent hiss,
For nectar's sweet, its nemesis.

Through sunlit hours, it roams the field,
In search of flowers that won't yield.
A bitter chase, a fleeting kiss,
Forever bound to nectar's bliss.

When moonrise casts its silver hue,
The bee persists, the night its cue.
In moonlit blooms, it finds amiss,
The haunting taste of nectar's kiss.

The dance, eternal as the sky,
The bee and bloom, forever tied.
A love, a curse, an endless miss,
The tale of nectar's nemesis.

As dawn returns, so too the fight,
In bloom's embrace, in morning light.
The bee resumes its endless tryst,
Forever chasing nectar's mist.

Milton Keynes UK
Ingram Content Group UK Ltd.
UKHW010804220824
447080UK00005BA/70

9 789916 863794